"This book would also animal lover will appreciate this heart-felt story."
—*Stephanie Chandler, author and animal rescue advocate*

"One cannot script who will leave a forever touchstone in one's heart. In Horse at the Corner Post, author Denise Branco vividly and emotionally captures a lifelong friendship with a special horse named Freedom Sky. You will find yourself captivated by this special friendship story between a young woman and a young colt and what transpires during the next three decades. For anyone lucky to have had a heart connection with a pet, I urge you to read this book. Branco gently and lovingly leads you by the reins to a destination we all cherish – a tale of forever love and friendship."
—*Arden Moore, pet author, editor, and founder of Four Legged Life, a pet community.*

"Horse at the Corner Post is an honest story of not only the special bond between a girl and her horse, but also the wonderful love between a girl and her parents. The story of Denise and Freedom inspires me to enjoy every moment and relish the fulfillment from having a special animal to love. The story is genuine and endearing."
—*Jeffrey Schmidt, DVM, Arbor View Veterinary Clinic*

HORSE

at the

CORNER POST

Our Divine Journey

BY DENISE LEE BRANCO

To Lisa,
Such a pleasure
meeting you. I hope you
enjoy riding along on my
divine journey. Denise Lee
Branco
7/14

Horse at the Corner Post: Our Divine Journey
By Denise Lee Branco
1. Pets: General 2. Religion: Inspirational 3. Biography & Autobiography: Personal Memoirs
ISBN: 978-0-9845888-0-0
Library of Congress Control Number: 2010914062
Cover design by Lewis Agrell

Printed in the United States of America

Published by
Strolling Hills Publishing
395 S. Highway 65, Suite A-119
Lincoln, CA 95648
www.StrollingHillsPublishing.com

Please visit: www.HorseAtTheCornerPost.com

This book is dedicated to my parents.

Mom and Dad, I love you more than words can express.

&

In memory of my beloved horse, Freedom.

May 20, 1976 – January 27, 2008

Table of Contents

Author's Note

This is not just a story about a horse; it is a story about a special bond between two best friends: one, two-legged; the other, four.

In 1993, family and friends urged me to write about the miraculous events surrounding my beloved horse, Freedom. I did, in fact, write a short story at the time, and while read and enjoyed by some, it simply became a treasured keepsake, filed away in a desk drawer.

It wasn't until Freedom's passing that it occurred to me: the story of my life with Freedom was finished—

from beginning to end. At that moment, I felt a huge need to write about our unique connection.

Writing turned into therapy for me. I didn't realize how much I needed to express my feelings in order to cope with my loss. I couldn't believe how much of my heart had poured out onto the pages as I chronicled our lives over the past three decades.

The last thing I want is for this book to be dismal. I want it to be a celebration of Freedom's life. Please note that all humans in this story have been given character names, while all horses' names are authentic.

Come along on my journey and join me in paying tribute to my dear equine friend, Freedom.

In the Beginning...

May 20, 1976

It was a year packed with events celebrating the United States of America's Bicentennial. Freedom '76 slogans briskly swept through America while red, white, and blue trios sparkled across the land. Old Glory elegantly waved with each subtle breeze.

American pride—we all had it. I was a youth and had convinced myself that my collection of commemorative coins and two-dollar bills would, one day, be worth millions. Instead, I learned that the most valuable things in life have nothing to do with money.

I was born into a long line of cattle ranchers. My parents brought me up with old-fashioned country values and plenty of animal friends.

We had just one brood mare named Barred's Sky. Her sorrel coat glistened, and a distinctive blaze marking of white hair traveled down her forehead. She walked about with an inevitable sway in her back and a protruding belly after carrying foals to term for many years.

On May 20, 1976, a fresh soul arrived on Earth—birthed without complications. Proud mother Barred's Sky nudged her new addition to stand within hours. His lanky legs trembled as if he were high atop stilts. He gained strength and soon dashed to every corner of the field.

The foal's mother and father were registered in the American Quarter Horse Association (AQHA). Carrying on the tradition of registering him was both important and honorable. As a tribute to his mother and the historical year commemorating American freedom, my parents registered the foal as "Freedom Sky." But, he needed a nickname—something to better describe his little independent personality. The logical conclusion hit me—"Freedom."

Three Days Old

T he newborn lay on a blanket of clover, enjoying warmth from the morning sun and clueless as to what was going on around him. I tiptoed my way into his paddock and knelt down beside him, gently stroking his neck as he continued to bask. He'd open his eyes momentarily and then fall back into a deep sleep.

Freedom showed no fear at his first human encounter. Slowly and gently, I slid a foal-sized nylon halter over his head, and carefully buckled it. He lounged and every so often lifted his head high enough to see that his mother was nearby as I caressed his velvety hair. Before he could realize what was happening, I scooted under him so that when he lowered his head, his head landed in my lap. He seemed unconcerned. The natural instinct to fear strangers could have triggered the need to bolt. It didn't; Freedom trusted me.

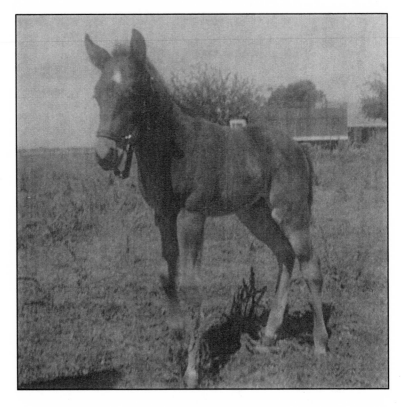

Confidence and pride emerged as he stood to model his blue halter. He remained beside me while enjoying his newfound attention. I wanted my mom to witness

Freedom's milestone. I yelled, "Mom!" a couple times and watched as she rushed to the fence, expecting some sort of danger with me being in the middle of a mare and her newborn. As soon as she saw Freedom standing next to me, her worried look disappeared.

Freedom had his first photo shoot that day—never once flinching from clicking camera sounds. After snapshots were taken, Freedom walked over to his mother's side, and I went into the house to brag about his accomplishment.

Looking back, it was a defining day in my life. Freedom and I connected, soul to soul. It was the beginning of a bond that would last for decades.

Let's Race!

Barred's Sky and Freedom grazed their way around my parents' twenty-acre ranch in Merced, California. They seemed to especially enjoy the northwestern corner of the ranch. The fence bordering the ranch was made of wire connected by fence pickets and wooden corner posts. The wire stretched along a paved public road, a tomato farm's dirt road, a neighboring pasture, and our backyard.

A stocky, yet cunning, twenty-year-old Quarter Horse gelding named Bill also lived at our ranch. Three halters were no match for this magician. If he was tied to the trailer awaiting a ride, Bill would inevitably rub off all three halters. He wouldn't go far, though; his destination was always the closest food source.

We adopted Bill from my uncle Zack three years prior to Freedom's birth. When Uncle Zack's horses were too old for the physical demands of rodeo competition but still young enough to ride for pleasure, he often sent them to our ranch for us to enjoy and for the horses to live out the rest of their lives.

Bill most likely would not hurt Freedom, but it was best to keep them separated until Freedom grew older. So, my parents created a one-acre paddock with fence wire at the northwestern corner of the field for Barred's Sky and Freedom. It wasn't long before the two had carved dirt trails into the pasture along their favorite routes. The most traveled trail led to the corner fence post between the paved public and dirt farm roads.

Cowboys rode horseback to round up cattle and herd them into corrals a half mile away. I could barely see the distant silhouettes, but Barred's Sky seemed quite entertained by them. Freedom soon learned his mother's ways. The pair were often seen at the corner, alert and standing side-by-side or napping upright, positioned nose to opposing tail for fly-swatting ease.

I was a girl and Freedom was a foal. That

combination meant a surplus of energy between us. I remember feeling sorry for Freedom, because he didn't have other foals to play with. So, I taught him to race— with me.

After school and on weekends, I ran outside the fence along the public road and shouted, "Come on, Freedom! Come on!" Digging his hooves into the ground, he sprinted to the end of the field and glanced over at me for clues as to how long the challenge would last.

Freedom always enjoyed our playful ritual. The way he sprinted feverishly and waved his tail in the wind after he crossed the imaginary finish line was all the proof I needed.

Spring of 1977

The Blue Roan

As the seasons changed, so did Freedom's coat of hair. A blue roan emerged as speckles of bluish-grey strands grew within his velvety-brown hair.

Almost a year had passed since Freedom's birth, and it was time for his mother's next foal to come into this world. My parents moved Barred's Sky to the larger field to wean Freedom from her. Since Freedom was older now, Bill could share the one-acre paddock with him, and so, the two became "roommates."

Freedom had just graduated from his blue, foal-sized halter to a red, yearling-sized one. My goal was to prepare him for a horse show career, because I loved the sport of showing horses.

We spent many hours in his paddock practicing horse show skills. One of the most important practice lessons involved picking up and setting down Freedom's hooves one by one and then repeating this ritual. The purpose was two-fold: handling his hooves would calm him for the blacksmith, and teaching him to "square-up" (stand motionless with all four hooves placed in a square shape) would be a critical showmanship necessity to compete successfully in equestrian events. Another lesson involved placing barrels in his field to familiarize him with future barrel racing competitions. He did, in fact, discover the cloverleaf pattern arrangement of barrels in his field, but instead of walking around and studying them as he was supposed to, they became the perfect itch-scratching objects.

Freedom reached the age where he was able to learn things best taught by a professional. My parents sent him away for a few months of formal training to "accept" a bridle bit and rider, and to "load" into and "unload" from a horse trailer.

When Freedom returned to the ranch after weeks of training, he seemed so grown-up. A frisky, carefree colt had turned into a mature, confident horse. I was overjoyed and thought, "Finally! I can ride him, and together, we can discover new things!"

August 10, 1980

Kindergarten Pleasure

I was chomping at the bit to enter Freedom in a horse
show with other horses his age.

My uncle Lester called our home one day to invite
us along to an out-of-town horse show. Uncle Lester had
noticed an event on the show's registration form that
was specifically designed for young horses. He thought
we might be interested—and he was right! What a thrill
it would be to show Freedom at his first competition.
The event had a fun name, too: Kindergarten Pleasure.

I remember that day, August 10, 1980, as if it were

yesterday. The horse show grounds hid in a clearing of tall pine trees in the sparsely populated mountain town of Mariposa, California.

Once we arrived and got the horses "show-ready," I began my own pre-event routine. The "usual" meant buckling on suede chaps, slipping on white gloves, and wrapping hair into a bun underneath a cowboy hat. My mom helped me pin the day's entry card to the back of my western shirt. That day, my number was "95."

An entry number promotes fairness among competitors by keeping names anonymous. The judge makes a decision based on horse and rider skills. The show announcer, in the arena booth, announces names at the end of the event.

Typically, at Western Pleasure horse shows, horse and rider circle the arena at a stride instructed by the judge. Competitors wait for the judge's request to walk, trot, lope, or to reverse the direction to clockwise, stop, and move backwards.

I have past experience with showing horses. I know what is expected; Freedom didn't. I was determined to show Freedom at his best. We walked out into the arena and began our counterclockwise circle. I noticed there were only five other competitors. Odds were in favor of us, as long as Freedom remembered cues from our practice sessions.

At home, Freedom stood for hours in his paddock monitoring changes in the world around him. He often came up to the backyard fence to watch our house and driveway for any signs of people or family pets moving about.

Nothing was different at his first horse show. Even though I sat straight in my saddle in showmanship posture, concentrating on displaying effortless technique, Freedom often forgot to pay attention to the inside of the arena.

Almost from the start, Freedom's ears were turned forward and his eyes were fixed on everything in the distance. He always stayed in proper stride and followed every cue, but he needed an occasional gentle reminder tap on the reins to focus. It was easy to regain his attention, but it only lasted a few minutes. His failure to remain attuned to the task at hand could affect our final score.

When the horse show judge finished evaluating all individual competitors, he asked each competitor to ride to the center of the arena for additional judging. The judge observed each rider's ability to square-up his or her horse. Once done, he proceeded down the line of competitors to test each rider's ability to back his or her horse.

Riders who can back their horse with the least

amount of effort are usually the most impressive to
a judge. The judge nods to the rider to stop backing
and return to that rider's place in line. He then walks
around the line of horses to observe from behind. Of
concern is whether a horse will get nervous when a
stranger stands or walks behind him. A horse's natural
instinct to fight or flight may kick in at any time.

Luckily, in our case, Freedom remained calm and
composed during that phase. The judge finished circling
our line. I watched as he walked to the announcer
with his clipboard list of winners. I felt confident the
judge noticed that Freedom mastered every command,
but his inattention may have cost us points. I focused

entirely on my horse during the competition and was unaware of my competitors' performance. The only thing I noticed was that Freedom was the tallest, largest kindergartener.

I have found that most judges prefer horse and rider remain in competitive form the whole time during the event. Even when my competitors and I were asked to line up for an individual review, I cued Freedom to remain standing squared-up while I sat straight in the saddle—just in case the judge glanced our way. We stayed in competitive form, not relaxing for even one second.

Ribbons were awarded to the fifth place. I believed we had a good chance to get at least fifth place. The instant I heard the overhead speakers click on and the announcer's voice, I couldn't control the butterflies.

The announcer began reading the list of horse and rider winners. He read the name of the fifth place winning duo. It wasn't us.

Then, the fourth place winner. It still wasn't us.

Then, third place. Still—not us.

Do we even have a chance? A chance at first place, I wondered? Or, maybe we placed sixth and would not get a ribbon at all. I had two ounces of optimism mixed with one ounce of pessimism.

Then, I heard over the loud speaker, "*Second place*

goes to Denise Branco and Freedom Sky." SECOND! How wonderful! Our first horse show and we placed second!

I gave Freedom a loving pat on the side of his neck, and we walked up to the judge to receive our red ribbon. I was so proud of Freedom.

After the event, my parents asked the judge for feedback. He told them that I did my best to maintain control of such a large horse, and we performed well in all categories. However, due to Freedom's interest in activities around the show grounds, the judge could not award us a first place ribbon.

Even though we did not win first place, I was completely satisfied with Freedom's debut horse show performance and content with our second place ribbon. Little did I know at the time that it would be our first and last horse show.

I will always be grateful for the excitement and fond memories of that day. I still have that red ribbon and our number "95" entry card. I treasure them today, more than ever.

Bye for Now

I'm sorry to say that I spent less time with Freedom as I neared my college years. Schoolwork and hanging out with friends occupied my time. It may seem odd, but I clearly recall feeling that I was keeping a great horse from a fulfilling life. He deserved to be ridden and experience different things.

Freedom's large frame was perfect for sprinting, a plus for timed scores at calf-roping events. Experienced horsemen reinforced my parents' concern that I might not be able to control Freedom if he got scared, since he was so big and powerful. Uncle Zack was an active rodeo competitor and interested in Freedom. It seemed only logical that he take Freedom in trade for his smaller, older black horse. At least we would always know where Freedom was.

It was only because I felt rodeo life was best for Freedom and I loved watching movies and reading books with black horses that I agreed to the trade and Freedom left our ranch. At the same time, I expected to get Freedom back from my uncle one day when Freedom was too old to compete in rodeos but young enough to enjoy riding—just like all the other horses that my uncle had retired to my parents' ranch.

Soon after Freedom left the ranch, the black horse misbehaved. Tied to the barn and waiting to be ridden one day, the black horse pulled back on his halter rope with all his strength and yanked out several planks of wood.

His demeanor never calmed, and it wasn't long before my parents found another home for the black horse. At that point, I decided that I did not want to ride any horse if it couldn't be Freedom.

Spring of 1988

Chance Meeting

The years rolled by. It was spring of 1988, and I, like so many other spectators, traveled to the rodeo grounds in Chowchilla, California for their annual Stampede rodeo. While my parents and I sat in the grandstand, we heard my Uncle Zack's name over the loud speaker as a competitor. We hadn't seen Uncle Zack in years and went looking for him.

When we finally found Uncle Zack, it was just like old times. Mutual happiness was shared between us all as we chatted for a few minutes. Out of the blue, Uncle

Zack told us that Freedom was at the rodeo that day. Without hesitating, he said he'd find Freedom's owner before the next event.

What? Uncle Zack was not Freedom's owner? We were in a state of shock at that moment and couldn't believe that Freedom no longer belonged to my uncle. He never told us Freedom had been sold.

I stood in anticipation waiting for Freedom. Saddled and led by his owner, Freedom made his way to me. How wonderful it was to see him again. I petted Freedom while my family and I talked with his new owner. Thank goodness he was such a nice man. I was thrilled when he suggested I take Freedom for a short ride around the rodeo grounds.

Aside from an occasional trot, we mostly walked. I wanted to take it all in—to enjoy a leisurely ride for what little time we had together. Freedom would often stop in his tracks, turn his neck, and smell my boot. I believe he was trying to convince himself that it was me. After all, I was older and no longer the teenager he knew.

Although I had goals to achieve and not much time to ride, I wished I had Freedom in my life again that day. I regret not asking his owner to consider selling Freedom to me. Instead, I assumed that his owner didn't want to sell Freedom since he had just bought him from my uncle.

I did not ask Uncle Zack why he sold Freedom. I figured it was water under the bridge at that point. My uncle is a professional cowboy, and I don't blame him at all for wanting to continuously improve his competitive edge with better horses.

I am grateful for the blessing I received that spring day when our paths crossed. It was only for a few hours, but I have never forgotten the joy of seeing Freedom after so many years. Sadly, the day came to an end, and I had no choice but to go on with my life without Freedom.

Winter of 1992

Hoping for a Miracle

During the winter of 1992, I wanted to return to my true passion in life—horses. I searched for available horses for months but couldn't seem to find the right match.

One weekday morning, I awoke startled and worried. I dreamt that Freedom was in danger. I had not seen this horse in years, and out of the blue, his presence overcame me. I didn't know what kind of danger but was horrified when I saw him in my dream being taken away in a horse trailer, destination unknown.

Before showering, before even packing my lunch, I called my mom. I was living in Sacramento, California at the time, and my parents still lived on the ranch in Merced. My mom picked up the phone, and I told her, "Mom! I dreamt Freedom is in danger, and I need to find him!"

Stunned, my mom replied with only one word, "What?" We hadn't talked about Freedom in years. Understandably, my mom was silent and in shock as I explained the details of my dream to her.

That evening, I phoned my parents again and shared the details of my dream with my dad. I found myself telling him about it with much more urgency. It was very important to me not to waste any more time. We needed to find Freedom!

The following day, my dad phoned Uncle Zack and asked him to use his contacts within the rodeo circuit to locate Freedom. Later that week, Uncle Zack called to report that Freedom had been sold again, and his whereabouts were unknown. My uncle's last words to my dad were, "You'll never find that horse." That statement made me even more determined and angry over the negativity. I can understand that to some it may seem impossible, but I was going to find Freedom! That's all there was to it!

I decided to write to AQHA and request a current

ownership trace. I assumed it would take time to research, but it didn't. Their response arrived in a matter of days.

As I pulled the letter out of my mailbox, the sender's name leaped off the envelope. AQHA! I tore open the envelope and lo and behold, my dad was listed as Freedom's current owner. Amazing! But at the same time, it was another dead end.

I hurried to the phone and called my dad. After reading AQHA's response to him, I pleaded that he call Uncle Zack once more. I reminded him, "We have to find Freedom! He is in danger!"

After a little persuasive nudging, my uncle agreed again to help track down Freedom. He told us he would locate the man he had sold Freedom to and ask for leads.

We all waited for things to fall into place. My aunt Patty suggested we pray to St. Anthony, the Catholic saint who helps you find things lost. I was willing to try anything. We heeded my aunt's advice and began our prayers to St. Anthony.

* * * * * * * *

Two weeks to the day, my parents received a call from Uncle Zack. He believed that what he referred to as the "roan horse" was boarded at stables in San

Luis Obispo, California. Uncle Zack gave my parents the owner's name and phone number. It was the best lead we had had in weeks! A click, a dial tone, and the numbers of hope catapulted through a phone line to the home of a man named Garrett.

The horse's description seemed to match Freedom perfectly. Garrett even commented, "I think it's the horse you're looking for." We were hopeful, yet cautious. Could it be him? Were our endless prayers to St. Anthony about to be answered?

I would have scored the fastest time at a luggage-packing contest that evening if one had been held. I was out the door and on my way to my parents' home before the end of the evening news. This trip to San Luis Obispo had to be a success. It just had to be! I could not accept another dead end. Time was running out to find Freedom! I couldn't stop believing that he was in some sort of danger.

Reunited

I struggled to control my excitement as each minute passed. My heart pounded as our truck edged its way down the boarding stables' entrance in San Luis Obispo, passing horse corrals to an open parking area. When the truck finally crept to a stop, I jumped out to scan the property for Freedom.

No one needed to identify him to me. My eyes stopped at one horse standing in the midst of a group of horses. No doubt, it was Freedom! Feelings of joy, gratitude, and excitement all surfaced. The journey of dead ends and hope led to that exact moment of faith in finding Freedom.

A tall, lean man in his sixties seemed to appear out of nowhere. He introduced himself to me and my parents as Garrett. I knew it was important to be polite and get to know Garrett, but I couldn't help but watch Freedom moving about in his corral.

Garrett told us that he had owned Freedom (whom he called Roanie) for a few years and had some success at roping events. He explained that he had been battling cancer, and his declining health made it difficult for him to ride. Garrett spoke about his aspirations of riding Freedom along the Pacific Ocean. For thirty consecutive days, he rode Freedom on the beach. Freedom feared the crashing sound of ocean waves the entire month and never calmed.

We followed Garrett over to the adjoining corral where a twenty-two-year-old sorrel Quarter Horse gelding named Fifty-Two stood and watched us approach. Tossing a section of mane over the horse's neck, Garrett disclosed white hair perfectly shaped into the number "52," evidence of the horse's previous military service. He explained that Fifty-Two served in the mounted police unit at a nearby military camp in the 1980's.

Finally, after all the introductions and storytelling,

I received the best offer ever. Garrett suggested I take "Roanie" for a ride and then offered Fifty-Two to my dad to ride. He knew Freedom did not do well alone in wide, open spaces, and having another horse nearby would provide Freedom with a sense of security. It had been years since my dad rode a horse, and he was thrilled by this opportunity to ride again. His last special horse was Freedom's mother, Barred's Sky.

Garrett escorted us to the tack compartments of his horse trailer, turned to my dad and said, "Here. Here's the key. Help yourself any time you want to ride." Garrett's kind soul shined. How many people give you free access to their belongings when you've just met? I suppose Garrett sensed my tremendous joy at being reunited with my horse.

Before our ride, I leaned over in front of Freedom's nose so that he could smell my head. My hope was that the scent of my hair might trigger his past memories. This lasted a few minutes, as it seemed he was putting the pieces of the puzzle together in his mind.

When I stepped up into the saddle, I noticed Freedom slowly turn his head to the left and stretch his nose to my cowboy boot. He stopped and rested his nose against my boot for a few moments, inhaling and exhaling. I believe he was rewinding the memories of his life.

I never once called him Roanie. Freedom was his name, and even if I had to whisper it when Garrett was nearby, I called "my horse" by his name. He listened closely and I am convinced that in all those years, he never forgot his name was Freedom.

This was a day to get to know each other again. Nothing more desired than a slow-paced, take-it-all-in day. One would anticipate much activity where several horses are housed, but on this particular weekend day, the arena was ours—just Freedom's and mine. My parents looked on, perched up on wooden arena fence boards. No other horses, no other riders. We walked, trotted, loped, and even pretended we were professional barrel racers.

My parents noticed three barrels outside the arena and moved them inside for us, placing the barrels in the typical competitive cloverleaf design. Freedom moved through the course without any problem and after rounding the final barrel, seemed to enjoy sprinting to the finish line the most.

I wondered if Freedom would follow me without coaxing like he did years before. I decided to experiment. Dismounting and leaving the reins over Freedom's neck in the ready-to-ride position, I walked forward. It could have been a long shot, but I knew Freedom, and I had faith he would follow.

He did! Saddled, bridled, and rider-less, he followed me without any hesitation. I jogged—he trotted. Facing my back, he followed me the whole time. I trusted him despite what could have been a dangerous situation. I knew my horse would never intentionally hurt me.

We spent a few hours in the arena riding and merely standing around. That's what I mostly wanted to do: live in the moment, just spend time with Freedom— pet his silky hair, talk to him, and take more photos. I was overjoyed each time I walked around and Freedom followed me without any coaxing.

The bond was still there. I have no doubt that he knew me and my parents. I feel sure he remembered we were the family that cared for him when he was young.

I noticed that a dirt road branched off from the boarding stables and wound its way along a rocky mountainside. A scenic trail ride before we left seemed like the perfect way to end the day. So off we went.

Dad and I had only ridden the horses a few yards up the road when an opening in the dense brush stopped us in our tracks. Instantly, we were mesmerized by the view. Lush grass blanketed across miles, and communities sprouted over the valley floor and foothills. Beauty, peace, and sanctity—only a taste of what might appear over the ridge.

It was already late afternoon. The sky darkened, and the wind blew stronger. We decided it was time to turn the horses around and head back down the road. It had been a day chockfull of quality time.

Once we returned to the horse trailer, I replaced Freedom's leather bridle and reins with a nylon halter and rope, removed his western saddle and saddle blanket, and spent time brushing his hair and combing his mane.

The most difficult part of the day came when it was time to leave. I was so engrossed in each moment that the thought of the day ending never crossed my mind.

It took all my effort just to walk Freedom back to his corral. I opened the wooden corral gate, led him in, and removed his nylon halter. I turned, as my eyes welled with tears, and walked back through the corral entrance. I exited the corral, shut the gate, stopped, and looked back at Freedom. I will never forget that moment. Through my watery blur, I saw Freedom staring at me. Standing there alone in the center of the corral, he had not moved an inch from where I left him. I sobbed all the way to the truck.

The highs of the day then became my lows. Having to leave Freedom behind broke my heart. Even though I couldn't help but call him "my horse," there was no guarantee he would ever again be my horse. I could only count on Garrett's offer to ride any time and to look forward to my next reunion with Freedom.

Voices Echoed from the Ridge

Three weeks never seemed so long. I could finally break away from the responsibilities of daily life to travel the distance to visit Freedom.

My parents and I met Garrett at the boarding stables for another weekend ride. This time, I brought along old photos of Freedom. I wanted Garrett to see how important Freedom was to me, and how proudly he stood next to me when he was just three days old. I wanted to touch Garrett's heart—to show him my love for Freedom was sincere. He smiled but seldom commented as we took the photographic stroll down memory lane.

Dad and I saddled up the horses and this time opted for a trail ride first. I felt such peace being with Freedom. I believe he shared my happiness at being together again. It was as if we were never apart.

As we rode further up the same dirt road from our last visit, we started hearing people talking in the distance. Tall brush surrounded each side of the roadway, so we could not see anyone. Dad and I looked at each other, puzzled. Every few feet, we'd pause, listen, and compare notes. Neither one of us could figure out where the voices were coming from.

Fifty-Two remained calm, but Freedom began to

prance. Suddenly, the sound increased and drew our attention upward, where we saw climbers scaling the rocky mountainside. Not wanting to push Freedom into a scary situation and unsure exactly how he'd react if we proceeded forward, Dad and I turned the horses around and headed back to the stables, opting to ride in a safer location—the arena.

Garrett returned at the end of our visit, as if he had timed it perfectly. Aside from asking if we enjoyed our day, his only other question was whether we had reached the top of the mountain ridge. I explained to him that Freedom's nervousness over the rock climbers' voices, and then seeing them on the mountainside, prevented us from reaching that goal. Garrett replied with composed optimism, "Maybe next time."

What a View!

F reedom was always on my mind as time crawled between visits to San Luis Obispo. The third visit with Freedom brought hopes of making it to the top of the mountain ridge. This day, for some reason, Freedom seemed calmer and more content.

Our ride began as usual. Dad on Fifty-Two and me on Freedom. But in a matter of minutes, we heard voices from rock climbers scaling the mountainside. Freedom listened, looked up and noticed the rock climbers, and continued on. Both horses seemed comfortable with

their surroundings and walked along unconcerned.

It was as if we entered another world once atop the ridge. The panorama went on for miles. Sunlight peeked through clouds shaped like cotton over the rolling foothills. The sun's warmth and a cool, gentle breeze were the perfect combination as we admired God's country. Just over the ridge, a galvanized livestock trough held water—a much-needed refreshment for the horses.

When we returned to the stables, I was surprised to see Garrett waiting. He greeted us with the same question: "Did you make it to the top?" This time, I replied with an excited "Yes, we did!"

Garrett had ridden that trail, and he knew the beauty beyond the ridge. He had a smile from ear to ear, not simply because we made it over the ridge, but because the rock climbers had not frightened Freedom. Most importantly, I believe he needed proof that I had the skills to guide Freedom to the ridge despite obstacles. It took one more week before his one and only pressing question made sense to me.

Memorial Day Weekend,
1993

Red, White, and Blue

F riday morning before Memorial Day weekend, 1993, began with an unexpected call. The caretaker of the boarding stables in San Luis Obispo phoned my dad. He asked if we were still interested in buying Freedom. I'd hoped for that moment for so long. "Yes!" The answer was also automatic for my dad.

Freedom's selling price could have easily been inflated since it was obvious how much my family loved Freedom. Any seller would probably conclude that my parents and I would have scraped up the money to pay whatever amount. Instead, Garrett had set a reasonable price.

The caretaker went on to explain that he would handle the sales transaction, on Garrett's behalf, as it was too emotionally difficult for him.

"What's going to happen to Fifty-Two?" Dad asked.

"Why? Do you have an interest in him?" replied the caretaker.

"We do. Fifty-Two helps keep Freedom calm." The caretaker promised to check with Garrett and report back.

When my dad phoned me with the exciting news that Freedom was for sale, he voiced his concerns about traveling with a horse trailer on one of the busiest travel weekends of the year. He asked me if the trip should be postponed until the following weekend.

Not hesitating for even one second, I told my dad, "We are going!" I was afraid if we waited for the next weekend, Garrett might change his mind. I didn't want to take that chance. My efforts to remain the fastest luggage-packing-contest winner resumed, and I was on my way again to meet my parents for the trip to San Luis Obispo.

That evening, the phone rang. On the other end, a somber voice responded, "I checked with Garrett about Fifty-Two. He wants to give him to you. No charge. And since you asked to purchase Freedom's saddle, Garrett would like to give you the rest of both horses' tack." What? Fifty-Two and his tack for free? We were in disbelief at such generosity.

Fifty-Two was getting up in age, and Garrett must have sensed we would give as much tender loving care to Fifty-Two as we would Freedom. Garrett's health was deteriorating, and I think his decision to keep the horses together brought him peace of mind.

* * * * * * * * *

Our rig crawled to a stop at our usual parking spot near the stable stalls. A silhouette in the shadows set his wrought-iron rake against a stall door and sauntered towards us. Greetings between the caretaker and my dad were brief, followed by a quick hand-over of funds and an escort to Garrett's trailer.

It was a bittersweet day for me. My heart sank for Garrett and his loss. He had to say goodbye to two beloved horses and all that reminded him of those horses, as his health continued to worsen. In the midst of Garrett's sadness was my joy in having Freedom back. We asked the caretaker to share our heartfelt gratitude with Garrett. He agreed to do so but paused to tell us a short story about the horses.

The caretaker revealed that Garrett put Freedom

up for sale in December 1992. Garrett decided he didn't need Freedom, since he could no longer ride competitively, but that he would keep Fifty-Two and ride as long as his physical health allowed. A high price was set for Freedom because he was a well-trained roping horse. For no apparent reason, Garrett pulled the advertisement shortly after listing it, and made an abrupt decision against selling Freedom.

Coincidentally, my dream occurred in December 1992. I believe God touched Garrett's heart that month and asked him to wait. God had a much bigger plan in store and assured him that it was not the right time to sell Freedom.

I grabbed Freedom's halter and hurried to his corral to bring him home. Freedom was named partly in honor of the United States of America, and he returned to the ranch where he was born during his birth month and on a red, white, and blue patriotic weekend. It seemed so fitting.

Bringing Freedom Home

Home at Last

The first thing I did when we got back to my parents' ranch was take Freedom for a ride. We rediscovered the entire twenty acres, stopping at times to enjoy the scenery. I was curious to see how Freedom would react if we rode to the corner of the field where he and his mother spent many days. That was going to be my test—to see what he would do. Would it jog his memory? Had it been too many years?

As we approached the corner of the field, he became more alert. His ears turned forward to listen for objects afar as his eyes gazed in the same direction. I could barely identify people and animals moving about on a ranch a mile away, but Freedom sure spotted them. Nothing got past him.

Tranquility at its best; there was no need for me to speak. I took my boots out of the stirrups, swung them atop his shoulders, and eased myself into a much more comfortable position as we stood. It didn't take long before Freedom relaxed his rear leg, and my equine easy chair tilted to the right. Mutual respect and contentment—our bond strengthened once again. I believe he knew he was home.

Freedom probably could have stood at the corner until dark, but it had been a long day and it was time to turn in. After all, there would be many riding days ahead.

Let the Riding Begin!

N ow that Freedom was home, he no longer had to experience the confinement of a small, dirt corral. He had the freedom to graze green pastures. The same one-acre corner of the ranch that Freedom shared with his mother and Bill was now his paddock to share with Fifty-Two, who loved to eat and seemed ecstatic to be living on lush clover.

Soon after being reunited with my horse, I felt a sense of urgency. Too many years had passed—too many rides hadn't happened. Now, there was no time to waste. Spending time together and sharing memorable rides was of utmost importance.

My parents leased additional summer pasture for their cattle, three miles from the ranch. Because the property was close to the ranch, it was a riding destination each time I visited my parents. Riding on the property always made me feel I had just stepped onto a movie set portraying the Old West.

At the entrance, an old barn stood tilted towards the east, weathered grey and airy from fallen boards. North of the barn, a restored windmill kept water flowing into a cattle trough. Parallel rows of wild daffodils returned every spring along a path to where a house once stood.

Towering eucalyptus trees grew alongside the barn and extended through the middle of the property. Rows of trees also bordered the entrance and stretched down the main road. I'm told that these eucalyptus trees were planted in a specific pattern for the circus when it came to town and needed shade and shelter.

A wide variety of creatures inhabited the property. Kildee birds nested in the pasture and scurried out when anyone walked by. White cranes stood on their orange, toothpick-thin legs along the irrigation ditch and ever so gracefully flew off when disturbed. Squirrels hurried in and out of their burrows, and cottontail rabbits rushed to and fro. Buzzards sat in the eucalyptus trees and atop fence posts, just waiting for any opportunity to swoop down for food.

Freedom was usually spirited during rides on the property. It took all my strength to keep Freedom's reins taut and in check. Although Freedom was typically overexcited, Fifty-Two always looked straight ahead—except for one time.

In the neighboring field, a blend of mules and horses roamed. On one particular ride, a female mule kept following my dad and me as we rode our horses along the fence line.

Fifty-Two looked straight ahead and tried to remain focused on the ride, but the female mule's energy was too much for him. He couldn't help but turn his head every so many feet to glance over at her. Dad also noticed Fifty-Two's unusual interest in the mule. I couldn't help but revert back to a tone from the first grade and announce, "Fifty-Two has a girlfriend!"

It seems the female mule made a lasting impression on Fifty-Two. Each time we returned to the property for an afternoon ride, we caught Fifty-Two scanning the neighboring field for the female mule. It was somewhat comical that he definitely did not forget he had a girlfriend there.

My parents also owned foothill property in Mariposa County and moved their cattle to the foothills every winter to graze. This ritual kept their cattle healthy and away from the muddy fields in Merced.

The only access to the property from the paved road was by way of a winding dirt road with numerous steep inclines. Oak trees and jagged rock remnants from past gold mining expeditions bordered the roadway.

The first time Dad and I took Freedom and Fifty-Two to the foothills to ride, Freedom was nervous about his new adventure, and it showed. Every time I loosened the reins, I sensed he wanted to flee. I'm sure my tight hold on the reins didn't help matters.

Whether the land was flat or hilly, Freedom was energetic with each ride. There were moments he would relax when we stopped to enjoy the scenery, as long as Fifty-Two stood next to him.

Despite the ongoing battle to hold Freedom back and attempts to calm him, I told myself to be patient. I wanted to give him time to get used to his new life. Maybe with time he would no longer fear his surroundings.

The Day the Land Gave Way

I always had a desire to horseback ride near a lake in Folsom, California, where trails meander through oak trees. Horse and rider duos are close enough to the lake to capture its beauty, as jet skis dart across the water and motor boats hum in the distance. A walk through the rich landscape can bring with it much serenity.

One summer morning, Dad and I saddled and bridled our horses for a leisurely ride at Folsom Lake. That day began on a peaceful note. Only the sound of chirping birds masked the clacking of our horses' hooves as we strolled along the trails.

The sport of horseback riding, as life itself, can be unpredictable. Situations often present themselves as reminders of how life's course can be altered in an instant. Split-second decisions must be made when in an instant, the unexpected can occur.

Freedom and I lead the way through the trees, while Dad and Fifty-Two followed directly behind. After reaching the top of a small hill, the trail leveled onto a dirt road in a clearing of land. In that instant, Freedom's head rose to its highest position, his ears stiffened and aimed forward, and his body tensed.

Out of the afternoon haze, a fisherman appeared, carrying his tackle box in one hand and fishing rod in the other. As the fisherman neared, Freedom increasingly feared his approach. The fisherman seemed to not know how to handle this situation, because he did the absolute worst thing. He stopped! Then, Freedom stopped.

The fisherman stood a few feet in front of me to my left. At saddle-height to my right, I noticed a dirt embankment carved into the road. My intuition told me Freedom's mind was made up. He was going to get away from that fisherman—no matter what. This escape would mean climbing the dirt embankment, a height of which was well above Freedom's shoulder. There was simply no way Freedom could climb that embankment safely while I sat aboard.

Thoughts raced in my mind. *He'll fall backwards! He'll hurt himself!* Then, there was no other choice. It was time to BAIL!

I released the reins, leaned to my right, and feverishly clawed my way over to the top of the embankment. Halfway through my dismount, Freedom climbed the same embankment. In a blink of an eye, the land gave way. We both slid down with the dirt, falling to our knees. Freedom leaped up and bolted down the dirt road.

Adrenaline pumped through my veins. I jumped up and ran after him. Freedom galloped about a hundred feet when thoughts of solitude must have entered his mind. He stopped, whirled, and began trotting back to Fifty-Two.

I met him halfway, grabbed his reins, and walked him a few yards to calm him. He needed reassurance that all was well again in his world—that the fisherman was gone and Fifty-Two was close by.

Freedom trotted the entire ride back to the trailer, still nervous from his frightening experience. The peaceful day had turned into an adventurous summer ride. What could have been tragic ended without injury...or so I thought.

Horse Trainer Persuasion

For nine months, I hoped Freedom would calm down. Every ride was a prancing affair. He was afraid of the outside world. Perhaps because Freedom had lived in corrals for years and was ridden primarily at calf-roping competitions, he feared life outside his enclosed surroundings. Freedom needed training from an expert horseman.

My parents read a newspaper article about a unique horse trainer's book. The trainer's techniques described in the article appeared to be exactly what

Freedom needed, and the horse trainer, named Trace, lived just thirty minutes from Merced. Dad called Trace and scheduled a training session for Freedom and me.

The weather on our training day was absolutely ideal—comfortable and not a cloud in the sky. When we arrived at the ranch, Trace greeted us on his golf cart. He was an older man, and his golf cart assisted him in getting around the ranch when walking was just too difficult. I was honored to meet Trace in person. It was an even greater honor to have him train my horse.

The training session brought with it new surroundings for Freedom. As usual, he was overexcited. Trace first put Freedom in a round corral. He kept Freedom moving around in the corral by voice cues and waving an orange flag in the air. Freedom finally calmed and eventually stopped to await further instructions.

Next, it was time for the obstacle course. As Dad and Trace looked on, Freedom and I approached a row of tires and wooden planks. This would be interesting. Freedom would have to step in and out of tires and walk across a wooden bridge. I had never attempted anything like this before with Freedom. I expected Freedom to be afraid of the black rubber circles on the ground, but he wasn't. He walked methodically through each tire. Next, I felt sure the sound of his hooves on the wooden bridge would frighten him, but it didn't. Who was this horse? He wasn't the Freedom I knew.

We moved on to the next biggest challenge—water! Freedom feared water. He always shied away from touching any body of water. Those thirty consecutive days that Garrett rode him along the ocean near San Luis Obispo probably intensified his fear.

Trace first created a gallon-sized puddle of water.

He asked me to walk Freedom over to the puddle. Freedom was reluctant to stand in the water at first. It was hard to believe that a two-thousand-pound animal didn't want to stand in a gallon-sized puddle of water. With reassurance that everything would be alright, Freedom finally stood in the water.

We stepped aside while Trace added more water to the puddle. Repeatedly, we walked back into and out of the puddle. Finally, Freedom stood in the water while the puddle grew and flowed all around his feet. He didn't move an inch. Instead, he looked around with an air of confidence.

We returned to the beginning of the obstacle course and breezed through each challenge more than once. This day was a milestone in Freedom's life. In my eyes, he became a new horse.

Splashing Away

I was still adjusting to Freedom's newly discovered love of water. It was amazing to have witnessed the transition. In the heat of the day, Freedom would often nod his head up and down in his water trough to create his own "rain shower." He splashed and splashed until his head, chest, and front legs were drenched with water.

Freedom made me laugh each irrigation season. He seemed to intentionally pound the water during our rides on the clover pasture. His chest and underbelly were soaked by the end of the ride, not to mention my pants and boots. Of course Fifty-Two was always nearby for moral support, and he seemed to enjoy the residual shower received from Freedom's playful splashing.

At my parents' leased property, I once stopped Freedom in the middle of an irrigation ditch with the water level knee-high, just to see how he would react. Freedom stood calm and looked around, awaiting the next instruction. To experience each of Freedom's milestones was extremely gratifying. He had come so far.

As Freedom gained confidence, we moved on to practicing stepping over fallen eucalyptus trees with varying trunk and branch sizes. Cows had eaten away all the leaves from the fallen trees, and it was easy to see where to step over the trees. We extended our tree course to include water puddles of varying sizes to walk through or step over. Freedom and I ended up creating an obstacle course reminiscent of the course designed by the horse trainer, Trace.

I am shocked at how a half-day training session with an expert horse trainer could cure Freedom's fear of water, but it did. What was once something scary to Freedom—water—instead became something fun.

January 1, 1998

Somber New Year's Day

He was twenty-six years of age, but we considered him a young horse. Fifty-Two was basically a healthy horse, with only minor past ailments; however, he seemed a little less motivated to live with each episode he encountered.

Fifty-Two walked the trails of his pasture for years without incident. Early in December 1997, a deep cut appeared on Fifty-Two's left front hoof. Initially, the hoof injury was a mystery. Then one day, my mom and I noticed a rusty metal gate protruding from a cement irrigation pipe. Years of winter rain and summer irrigation had washed away the dirt around the irrigation pipe and exposed the rusted metal gate, which we believe more than likely injured Fifty-Two.

To monitor Fifty-Two's health around-the-clock, my parents brought him from the field to a sheltered corral near the house. They also brought Freedom from the field to an adjoining corral. Freedom's role was to give Fifty-Two the moral support he needed, just like all the times Fifty-Two supported Freedom.

Even though our long-time veterinarian from Atwater was called out to the ranch twice during the month to treat the hoof injury, Fifty-Two's overall condition worsened.

Fifty-Two was such an easy-going and loveable horse. I'm so glad I was spending the holidays that year at my parents' ranch, so that I could help them care for him. We pampered him as much as possible, blanketing him and placing piles of hay in front of him.

New Year's Eve arrived, and we were hopeful that Fifty-Two would somehow pull through—that he would fight to live on and not give up. Labored breathing and an almost nonexistent appetite were signs that his health continued to worsen.

In a far corner of his corral, Fifty-Two lay down to sleep on the ground near the fence. During the night, his legs slid and wedged under the fence. Lines in the dirt were evidence of a hopeless struggle to remove them from under the fence. Too weak to continue his fight to live, Fifty-Two passed on.

We began New Year's Day saddened by our loss. It broke my heart to watch Freedom pace nervously in his corral as he watched a lifeless Fifty-Two being removed from the adjoining corral. Freedom proved to me that animals mourn, too.

I saw such grief covering my dad's face that morning. I can only imagine how he must have felt, mourning the memories of good times and special moments with his equine friend. It would take ten years before I, too, would experience the same painful loss of a beloved horse.

Flying Objects

Fifty-Two provided safety and security for Freedom. Alone, Freedom's fears were intensified.

The first afternoon ride without Fifty-Two began under an overcast sky. I decided to take Freedom to the leased property for a leisurely ride and to practice stepping over the fallen eucalyptus tree obstacle course we had created. He enjoyed maneuvering through the obstacle course during our training session with Trace, the horse trainer, and I believe he had fun each time we revisited our own personal obstacle course.

After only a few minutes into our ride, Freedom stopped abruptly. He raised his head high, straightened his ears forward, and opened his eyelids so wide that the whites of his eyes showed as he looked towards the sky.

I followed Freedom's line of vision for signs of what was troubling him. In the far distance, an advertising balloon glistened, gaining height ever so gradually. Freedom's fear escalated, and I sensed it couldn't be controlled.

Wrapping my right hand tightly around the saddle horn and holding on to the reins with my left hand, I braced myself. I didn't know what for exactly, but I did know that Freedom was going to react.

I leaned forward in the saddle for balance just as Freedom reared. He dropped back to the ground, landing hard on his front hooves. I tried to encourage Freedom to walk forward by reassuring him that everything would be fine. It didn't work. He reared again.

All alone out in the open field, Freedom decided he was not going to move forward as long as that "object" was in the sky. I dismounted, pulled the reins over his head, and led him back to the horse trailer to return home. Freedom never once looked back at the balloon in the sky. I was not equipped with the knowledge to handle a large, fearful animal. It was important for me to end on a peaceful note, before either of us got hurt.

Although our ride probably totaled only fifteen minutes in duration, it ended peacefully and injury free. It was not a day to ride. We would just have to try again another day.

Are You Sure?

I will never forget Freedom's actions one day. I can still visualize what happened. It is one of my fondest memories of him.

For a few months, a chestnut Quarter Horse gelding named Toasty lived at our ranch. One day, Dad and I decided to trailer both horses to the leased property for an afternoon ride.

In my childhood, I was taught to load the heaviest horse on the left side of a two-horse trailer to equalize the weight, since roads typically slant to the right.

Because Freedom was much larger than his buddy, Fifty-Two, Freedom always loaded on the left side of the trailer. Toasty was smaller than Freedom but trained by his previous owner to load on the left side, since he had been the only horse in the trailer.

Before each riding excursion, I tied Freedom to the trailer so I could brush his hair and comb his mane. Sometimes, I saddled him before loading him into the horse trailer; sometimes, I didn't. It all depended on how quickly I wanted to start riding once we arrived at our destination.

Freedom was always easy to load into the trailer. I'd simply throw the halter rope over his neck, guide him to be in line with the back of the horse trailer, and let him loose. I expected him to understand what I wanted him to do. It was automatic. I just stood back and watched him load without incident.

Dad and I witnessed one of Freedom's most intelligent moments that afternoon. After I groomed and saddled Freedom, I threw the halter rope over his neck and pulled slightly on the rope clip, under the halter, to guide Freedom in the direction of the back of the horse trailer. I stood and watched as Freedom walked freely as usual. But this was the first time Freedom had had to travel with a different horse—a horse that would load only on a horse trailer's left side. This meant that

Freedom would need to load on the right side.

I waited and observed Freedom walk nonchalantly to the back door of the horse trailer. It was amazing to be present and experience his train of thought. Freedom stopped when he noticed that only the right trailer door was opened. He paused and slowly turned his head to look at me. I did not touch him or lead him into the horse trailer. I simply said, "It's okay, Freedom. Go ahead." He didn't hesitate at all. Instead, he eased his neck back to align with the doorway and entered the horse trailer.

He seemed to question the change in routine and believe I made a mistake. It was as if you could read Freedom's mind asking me, "Are you sure?"

Mom's T.L.C.

My mom says she is not a horsewoman, but I disagree. Even though she is intimidated by the size and strength of horses, she showed her love for Freedom in many ways.

Growing up on a small farm in Dos Palos, California, my mom's parents raised farm animals—chickens, rabbits, and cows—to feed their family of six. There was no such thing as horseback riding for pleasure; horses were needed to pull farm plows up and down crop rows instead. Large, muscular draft horses were the only horses my mom knew as a child. Their size was quite intimidating for a girl.

Although Freedom was a large, spirited horse, my mom set aside her fears and gave him the best possible care. Mom's actions in taking care of Freedom proved to me that she loved him, too. He was not just a horse to her—he was a member of the family.

When the weather warmed and flies multiplied around my parents' cattle ranch, my mom began her daily ritual. Every morning, Mom placed a mesh fly mask over Freedom's face and head, and she removed it every evening. People not familiar with horse care often asked her if Freedom could see through the mask. She explained that the mask was like wearing dark-tinted sunglasses. Freedom could see out, but no one could see in.

There was always a bottle of fly repellant leaning against a tree near Freedom's fence. Not only did Mom give Freedom his full-body spray of fly repellant each morning, she made sure he received a squirt of fly repellant each time he walked up to the fence with even one fly on him.

On hot summer days, my mom braided Freedom's mane. She felt it kept his neck cool. She often grabbed the garden hose and sprayed water all over Freedom's body as he stood untied near the fence. He must have enjoyed the cool water running down his body; otherwise, he could have easily walked away.

Mom always made certain that Freedom had clean water to drink. She checked his water trough daily and used a scouring brush to clean it and then fill it with fresh water when needed. Mom also kept watch on the quality of his food and his weight. When the pasture lacked the nutrients an older horse required in the winter, she and my dad fed Freedom alfalfa hay.

It was obvious to me that my mom did not need to ride Freedom to love him. She feared horses, in general, and stood on the outside of the fence most times when caring for Freedom; yet she spoiled him in many ways. She discovered that Freedom would not intentionally hurt anyone. I never asked her to do any of the things she did for Freedom. Her actions came from the heart, and I will be forever grateful to her for giving him such tender loving care.

I feel guilty for not boarding Freedom closer to my home and taking the responsibility for his care from my parents. I often discussed these feelings with my parents, and they reassured me that Freedom would not have been happy anywhere else. He lived at the ranch where he was born, and he was the *Number One* horse. Granted, he was the only horse on the ranch at that time, but he still received VIP treatment. Our belief was that we would notice signs of changing health more often than a stranger might.

Freedom was part of our family, and as most people feel, no one can take care of family better than family itself.

Lights, Tractors, Action

F reedom always needed reassurance. When he no longer had Fifty-Two around, he looked to humans for comfort. My mom tells a story about standing an hour in the chilly night air to console Freedom.

During hot summer months, neighboring farms plowed their fields and planted their crops at night. From the kitchen window one evening, my mom noticed Freedom's stiff silhouette facing the field next to ours. Through the open window's screen, she heard engines start up and saw rows of tractor lights and planting equipment turn on. People scurried about as they got in position to plant tomatoes. Their voices escalated and carried across the field.

Freedom began pacing along the fence by our house. Mom worried he would try to jump out of the field to get away. He was tall and the fence seemed like it would be a small obstacle in his way if he were to become overwhelmed with fear. Mom rushed outside, stood next to the fence, and consoled Freedom. She kept telling him that everything would be alright. Mom could pet him only during moments that he froze to stare at the tractors.

Freedom eventually calmed down and then walked closer to the end of his field to watch the farmers and tractors. Mom couldn't believe what she had witnessed. Shocked at Freedom's behavior, she said, "Gee, thanks, Freedom. I just stood out here an hour in the dark and you're okay with it now?" She chuckled and walked back to the house.

About thirty minutes later, my mom glanced out the kitchen window and saw Freedom's silhouette outlined by tractor lights. She couldn't believe that he was still standing near the end of the field, curious about all the action and at the same time forgetting that it had scared him just minutes earlier.

Leaving the Corner Post

It seemed the years flew by too quickly. Freedom reached the age where he could no longer carry the weight of a rider. Arthritis was setting in; you could see it. I can still picture him at the corner of his field on cold mornings. The dampness and frigid air were especially difficult for him. He would alternate lifting and setting down his hooves to alleviate the pain of standing.

I greatly missed our riding days, but I looked forward to our grooming sessions as much as I think Freedom did. No matter where he was in the field, I

called his name and he answered back. I would walk
out to wherever he was standing in the field and start
brushing his hair and combing his mane. There was no
need to halter and tie him to a post. He was not going
anywhere—he loved being groomed. It relaxed him,
especially on those warm, sunny days.

He often followed me back to the house when we
were finished, stopping at the fence only to watch me
walk to the haystack. He waited patiently with one
ulterior motive—he expected a treat of alfalfa hay. If
I didn't return promptly with a flake of hay, his high-
pitched neigh made it known, loud and clear, that I
needed to hurry back with his treat.

Anytime my parents and I walked into the yard and
Freedom noticed, he always had something to say. He
knew that a neigh, followed by a stare, would charm us
into giving him a flake of hay. He didn't give up easily.
If we got busy and sidetracked, he reminded us with a
more serious-sounding neigh that he was still waiting.

It got to where he had trouble jumping over a
small irrigation ditch in the field. I'd grab the tip of
Freedom's halter lead rope and jump across the ditch to
wait for him. As he aged, he became nervous about his
ability to jump. He would size up the width of the ditch,
hesitate a bit, and then leap high to clear the water,
overcompensating for the distance.

Once, as I waited for him on the other side of the ditch, I watched his large stature jump towards me. He could have easily plowed right into me. Instead, he stopped directly in front of me so that I could hug his neck. I knew he would never intentionally hurt me, but I couldn't believe that in a split second, I had a horse's neck in my arms!

Freedom obviously enjoyed his years out in the pasture. He spent many summers standing at the corner post, sporting a mesh fly mask and capitalizing on the breeze of passing cars a few feet away. But the cold and rain of winter eventually became too harsh for his aging body. Freedom needed shelter to shield him from the elements. He could no longer remain in the open. It was time for Freedom to leave his corner of the field.

Discoveries in the Maze

Freedom returned to the corral he once occupied next to Fifty-Two. A portion of the corral was sheltered and could protect Freedom from the elements. Openings were made in several adjoining corrals so that Freedom could have a larger space to move about. He enjoyed the challenge of winding his way through all the corrals, which my mom nicknamed "The Maze." He discovered that standing behind the old barn kept him warm on sunny but breezy days. He found that an old fig tree branch, hanging over the corral fence, was the perfect back-scratching tool.

During weaning season, calves lived in the maze of corrals. If Freedom wanted to stand in a shady, covered area jam-packed with calves, he walked unconcerned into the herd and purposely scattered all the calves. He had no intention of harming them. It was just that he was the largest, and he believed he was the boss.

It saddens me that he was often seen standing in the northwest corner of one corral, looking in the same direction that he had always looked from his corner of the field. I wonder what he thought. Did he miss his corner of the field? I can only hope that he understood our intentions.

Winter of 2007

Freedom's Last Winter

He had slowed down with age. Freedom could no longer move about as easily when his hind legs became increasingly difficult to bend. Our veterinarian came to the ranch every five or six weeks to give Freedom an injection, which seemed to relieve his arthritic pain. Even the blacksmith began putting horseshoes only on Freedom's front hooves. This method decreased the time Freedom had to raise his legs during the horseshoeing process and, hopefully, limited his pain.

Although I prayed Freedom would live many more

years, my parents began to prepare me for the future. Our veterinarian warned them that Freedom might not be strong enough to make it through another winter. He recommended feeding Freedom nutrient-enriched senior equine grain and covering him with a horse blanket. The nutrients in the grain would help warm Freedom's body internally and the blanket, externally. Our veterinarian also suggested hanging a heat lamp in Freedom's covered shelter. We heeded his advice, but there were challenges ahead.

Problems arose with the horse blanket. It buckled in the front and sometimes restricted Freedom while he lay on the ground. He had trouble using his front legs to push himself up to stand. There were times the blanket had to be unbuckled and removed while Freedom was on the ground, just so he could get up.

Freedom did not always stand near the heat lamp. Sometimes, he stood under his heat lamp; other times, he backed in and faced out, exposing his neck and shoulders to the cold weather. Perhaps he felt irritated by the heat lamp light or maybe it was simply something unfamiliar to him. He spent many winters in the open field without the luxury of heat.

My parents cut a small section in the plywood wall of Freedom's covered, three-sided shelter to create a hinged door. This way, they could keep his shelter as warm as possible and only open it briefly to feed him. Freedom loved his nutrient-enriched senior equine food so much that he started neighing as soon as he heard approaching footsteps. He could not see through the little door but was always standing in position, anxiously awaiting his grain, when the door opened.

I witnessed Freedom's worsening physical condition during my December visit to my parents' ranch. I spent my usual time grooming him, but I also noticed that he wasn't the same. His back hooves dragged slightly when he walked. His pace was slow and steady. I wanted him to follow and trot behind me as he had so many times before. I jogged a short distance in his corral, but he could only slowly follow. I thought maybe he was just tired that particular day. After all, he had kicked up his heels during my visit the previous month. I found out later that Freedom had just received another injection prior to my visit in November, which is why he felt so good then.

Nevertheless, Freedom was thirty-one years old. I didn't want to accept the fact that his body was weakening.

His Spirit Will Live On

January 27, 2008

It was a Sunday morning, and I should have been sleeping in that day. Instead, I awoke from a deep sleep at four o'clock. Dazed, I found myself rewinding a dream still fresh in my mind. I envisioned Freedom basking in the sun, resting on bright green clover in a pasture, with five or six horses grazing nearby. I convinced myself the dream was untrue as it did not make sense. After all, Freedom lived in a corral and not in a pasture with other horses.

Five hours later, my dad called to tell me that

Freedom had been lying flat on the muddy ground in his corral and was unable to stand. Our veterinarian arrived to give Freedom the same series of shots which, the previous four times that winter, had helped Freedom gain the strength to stand again. The prognosis on this day was the same as usual—Freedom would be able to stand within three hours. However, by noon, everything had changed. Freedom's physical condition was rapidly deteriorating.

My parents worried about me driving over two hours in bad weather to see Freedom, but I had to be there. If this was the end, I had to be with him to say goodbye. I was the first human he met in his life, and I wanted him to know I was there to comfort him in his last hours.

During the emotional trip to Merced, my morning dream came to mind. I finally understood its meaning. God was calling Freedom home. It was time for Freedom to return to lush pastures under sunny skies, where he would be healthy again to run and play with other horses.

When I arrived at my parents' ranch, I rushed over to Freedom as he lay on the ground. I held his head, stroked his face and neck, and told him how sorry I was for him. I couldn't hold back my tears throughout the last ninety minutes of his life. At one point, I noticed my tear disappeared into Freedom's eye. I felt so bad. I hoped the tear did not sting his eye. He looked right at me, and in that moment, I believe my tear touched his soul.

I held and kissed the side of Freedom's face. He lifted his nose towards my face twice as if to give me a kiss. It touched me deeply. I leaned down to his nose and gave him the two kisses he obviously wanted.

I cradled Freedom's head the whole time we were together. He lifted his upper body a couple times. I could tell he was trying with all his strength to stand, but his legs were so stricken with arthritis that it was impossible. I'll never forget how Freedom lifted his head, held it up for a second, and looked back at his hind legs. I believe he was trying to tell me that he wanted to stand but could not bend his legs.

My parents were with me and Freedom the entire time. Their hearts were breaking, too. Freedom was so happy during his retirement years, thanks to my parents' tender loving care. They built shelters to protect Freedom from the elements. They fed him food specifically for senior horses. It was difficult for all of us to say goodbye. It was hard to accept the fact that Freedom's mind was sharp, yet his body could go no more.

Our veterinarian returned just before dusk. Time

had passed so quickly since I arrived at the ranch earlier that afternoon. Although I have the utmost respect for our veterinarian, I hated seeing him return. I didn't want to accept what he represented—easing Freedom's pain once and for all. I asked him if it was true, that Freedom would not be able to stand ever again. I looked for an ounce of hope from him. He didn't speak. He simply gave an affirmative nod. Our veterinarian had become a dear family friend over the years, and I could tell he felt our pain as well.

As raindrops started multiplying and the sky darkened, I realized that allowing Freedom to continue to lie on the ground was unfair to him. It seemed so cruel. None of us wanted him to suffer. He had brought us so much joy over the years. My inner voice reassured me that despite my selfish need to keep Freedom in my life, his body could go no further; it was okay now to let him go.

I whispered in Freedom's ear that I loved him. I promised him that I would see him again one day in Heaven. I cradled his head and caressed his face while God called Freedom home.

Animal Angel

I t was a sleepless night. My heart ached as I relived that January day. I realized that I could no longer hear Freedom neigh, brush his silky hair, or comb his entire mane. I knew then that I would always have a void in my life from that day forward. I will never be able to erase the fact that I lost a piece of my heart in January, my birth month.

The drive back home to Roseville the next day brought back so many fond memories of Freedom over the years. In between the tears over his loss,

I remembered various things he did to prove his intelligence. I smiled as I recalled the day he slowly and inquisitively turned his head to me after my unusual trailer-loading request.

I thought about our rides over the years. We covered a lot of ground. We rode on clover pasture, in the foothills, and even lakeside. The details of the day the fisherman scared Freedom came to mind so easily.

I had flashbacks to his younger years. It seemed just like yesterday that he was three days old. Freedom had been a part of my life for many years. I never really thought about life without him.

Along the route home, I decided to stop at a fast-food restaurant for a cup of coffee and a restroom break. As I stepped out of my car, I heard a cat meowing. At first, I couldn't figure out where the meows were coming from. Then, I noticed a cat at the side of the building, looking at me and meowing.

I decided to just talk to the cat and keep walking to the restaurant since I already had cats of my own. But once inside, I couldn't stop thinking about the cat and felt strongly that I couldn't bear to leave it behind. When I came out of the restaurant, I decided I would rescue the cat and find a home for it. But there was no trace of the cat. I scanned the parking lot. Still no trace of the cat.

I started my car, and a thought crossed my mind. Could that have been an animal angel? Did God send an animal angel to reassure me that Freedom was at peace and happy in Heaven? I drove off with confirmed faith—Freedom was in good hands.

Forever Close to My Heart

M y heart still ached. I couldn't let go. A multitude of feelings were bottled up inside. Perhaps the written word could ease my pain and comfort Freedom's soul.

Dearest Freedom,

When I allow myself to think about how much I miss you and the void you have left in my life, I cannot hold back the tears. I realize that people usually outlive their dear animal friends, but there's deep emptiness in not being able to see you. I said your name over three decades of my life. As unrealistic as it sounds, I always thought you'd be around.

I have been blessed with many animal friends in my life, but you were unique. I had a connection with you since your wobbly foal legs held you up and until your aged arthritic legs no longer allowed you to stand. I will forever cherish memories of our youthful race challenges, especially how you pranced over the imaginary finish line, flailing your tail each time as you left me behind.

Traveling to the ranch on weekends just didn't seem enough, but I treasured every moment with you. You made me feel special in your eyes when the pitch of your neighing raised an octave higher each time you greeted me. I regret not having a ranch of my own where you could live, and where I could have seen you every day. But, I know you were in excellent hands with Mom and Dad. You seemed very happy and content to live out your life on the ranch where you were born.

You have no idea the impact you had on my life and the lives of others. A cashier at the local grocery store drove past you daily on her way to and from work and fondly spoke of watching you stand at the corner of the field. Family friends, not seen in years, stop us in town to chat and always talk about you. They reminisce about driving by our ranch as you stood at the corner post. Even people we meet for the first time knew you *before they knew us. "That's where the horse stood at the corner along the road," is the automatic reply, when we give them our street address.*

The loose bone fragment and meniscus tear were surgically removed from my right knee a few months after our fall that day at Folsom Lake, but my knee still aches on extremely cold winter days. I don't mind at all. Each subtle ache brings you back into my life and reminds me of the days we spent riding or just hanging out.

The silver-plated engraved plaque with your name remains glued below the left front window of the horse trailer, as it will always be your side of the trailer.

Your leather bridle and all three nylon halters— blue, red, and purple—hang displayed around my home, each with an energy that's full of memories from different times in my life. Mounted on a hallway wall, a shadow box showcases items of you—your last two horseshoes, a section of your mane, and a steel comb—all reminders of happiness, when you stood next to me and enjoyed our grooming sessions. Tremendous joy comes from something eloquently displayed within the shadow box—our only award—that red second place ribbon.

Freedom, you will never be forgotten and my wish is that our story will live on to encourage others to open their hearts and allow a pet into their lives, for the love pets give back is one-thousand-fold. I hope our story gives people the confidence to never give up. Finding you proved that anything can be achieved with hope, faith, and patience.

When God calls me home one day, I know you will be waiting for me at the Pearly Gates. I believe that you won't say anything; you'll just be standing motionless, while watching me approach. It will be reminiscent of the day we were reunited at the boarding stables in San Luis Obispo. The way you watched me leave when that day was over is the way I picture how you will greet me in Heaven. I will walk in and hug your neck. No words, only a soulful connection. This time, however, we will be reunited for eternity.

Until then, Freedom, I will always treasure how much you enriched my life and will hold fond memories of you close to my heart.

Love Always,

Denise

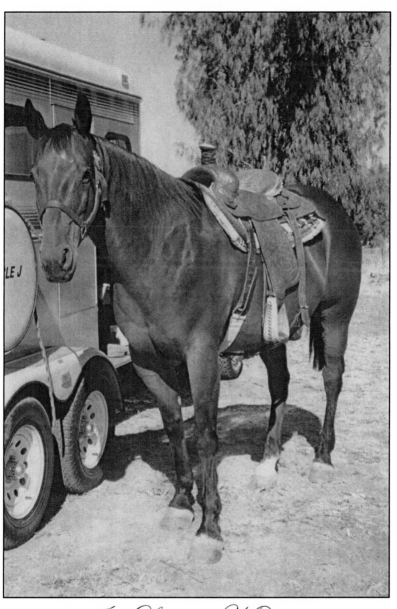

In Loving Memory
May 20, 1976 - January 27, 2008

Acknowledgements

I am blessed to have parents who have supported me in whatever I set out to accomplish. I could not have written this book without their continued encouragement during the process and assistance with recalling details from the past.

No words can describe the depth of gratitude I feel towards my parents for all they have done for Freedom, and for understanding the strength of my bond with him. I'll always treasure memories of happy times on our ranch and my many childhood animal friends. I hold my parents dear to my heart, as they are more than just parents; they are my confidants, my cheerleaders, and my friends.

Heartfelt appreciation goes out to cherished friends and family who witnessed my deep connection with Freedom and whose enthusiasm about my story, and belief in my ability to put it into words, kept me focused on reaching my finished product. Special thanks to Uncle Zack for being a vital part of my journey to bring Freedom back home, and to our outstanding veterinarian for helping us preserve Freedom's health as long as humanly possible.

I would like to thank fellow members of the Northern California Publishers and Authors (NCPA) and California Writers Club-Sacramento for their guidance and encouragement during an aspiring author's journey to share her story. Thank you for unselfishly offering your knowledge with such kindness. I have learned so much from you and will always be grateful for the friendships that I have gained from this experience.

A huge thank you goes out to my reviewers. You have no idea how sincerely touched I am by your beautiful endorsements.

Denise Lee Branco spent her childhood on a California ranch befriending all the furry and feathered residents there, but horses have been her greatest passion for as long as she can remember. From reading horse books to competing in western equestrian horse shows and Gymkhanas, Denise has always felt horses are a part of her identity.

As a youth, she wrote stories of her life, often signing the word "author" next to her name. But it wasn't until the passing of her most beloved horse, Freedom, in 2008 and Denise's reflection on their extraordinary connection that she felt compelled to pursue a writing career. She attended her first Northern California Publishers and Authors meeting one month after Freedom's passing and became a member shortly thereafter, and subsequently joined the California Writers Club-Sacramento Branch (CWC) in 2009. She also joined Toastmasters International in 2010. She currently serves on the CWC board of directors.

Horse at the Corner Post is her first book, and she hopes it will encourage pet adoption so that others can also experience the joy of a pet's unconditional love.